SAMPLERS

SUSAN MAYOR
AND
DIANA FOWLE

STUDIO EDITIONS
LONDON

PUBLISHED BY STUDIO EDITIONS LTD.
PRINCESS HOUSE, 50 EASTCASTLE STREET
LONDON W1N 7AP
ENGLAND

SAMPLERS
REPRODUCES A SELECTION OF SAMPLERS FROM THE SWAMETHAM
COLLECTION, LONDON; CHRISTIE'S SOUTH KENSINGTON;
CHRISTIE'S NEW YORK; THE VICTORIA AND ALBERT MUSEUM, LONDON

POSTER ART SERIES

SAMPLERS
IS A VOLUME IN THE POSTER ART SERIES.
UP TO TEN PLATES MAY BE REPRODUCED
IN ANY ONE PROJECT OR PUBLICATION,
WITHOUT SPECIAL PERMISSION AND FREE OF CHARGE.
WHEREVER POSSIBLE THE AUTHOR, TITLE AND PUBLISHER
SHOULD BE ACKNOWLEDGED IN A CREDIT NOTE.
FOR PERMISSION TO MAKE MORE EXTENSIVE USE OF
THE PLATES IN THIS BOOK APPLICATION MUST BE MADE
TO THE PUBLISHER.

ISBN 1 85170 368 3

PRINTED IN HONG KONG

INTRODUCTION

Some form of sampler must have existed since embroidery began. However, it is not until the early sixteenth century that such works are first mentioned by name. The earliest literary reference is found in an inventory of Elizabeth of York, wife of King Henry VII, dating from 1502, which mentions 'an ele of linen cloth for a sampler for the queen'. From this date onwards there are many written allusions to the sampler, which suggests that its use had become quite widespread, although relatively few sixteenth-century examples survive. In Shakespeare's *A Midsummer Night's Dream* Helena asks Hermia:

> O, and is all forgot?
> All schooldays' friendship, childhood innocence?
> We, Hermia, like two artificial gods,
> Have with our needles created both one flower
> Both on one sampler . . .

Skelton refers to 'a sampler to sowe on, the laces to embroide', and several wills of the period make specific mention of them.

The development of the sampler in the sixteenth century is directly connected with the rise in popularity of amateur needlework. An expanding economy and an increasingly luxurious life-style played their part in this, and the New Rich were eager to display their success through the lavishness of their possessions. Well-to-do ladies of leisure devoted much of their time to embroidery. 'Bess' of Hardwicke, Countess of Shrewsbury, was just one of a number of famous amateur needlewomen who were extremely skilled at their craft. She and her ladies embroidered many of the hangings at Hardwicke Hall themselves, although a professional embroiderer may have drawn the original plans. Women worked not only at household furnishings, but also on smaller-scale pieces, decorating items of costume or linen with embroidery.

For both the amateur and the professional adult embroiderer, the sampler offered a practical aid, since it was used as a form of notebook in which patterns and stitches could be recorded for future reference, rather than as a schoolgirl's exercise. Indeed, the word 'sampler' itself derives from the French '*exemplaire*', meaning a kind of pattern or model to be imitated; and it is interesting to note that John Palsgrave's Anglo-French Dictionary of 1530 contains an entry which reads 'examplar for a woman to work by, exemple'. The earliest known dated sampler of this kind was worked by Jane Bostocke in 1598 and is in the Victoria and Albert Museum (plate 1).

In the sixteenth century the shape of most samplers reflected their practical purpose. They were long, narrow rectangles, with one loom width of the linen cloth generally used for the length, which might be up to four or five times the width of the finished work. An example of a favourite border could then be sewn across the material, with space for at least one repeat of the design but without wasting cloth on unnecessary ornamentation. These 'long' samplers were often stored round an ivory rod or rolled up in a workbox, so that the embroideress could easily refer to them for inspiration while working on another article. In some cases they are worked from either end, with the result that some border patterns or alphabets appear upside down.

The necessity of creating such embroidered memoranda diminished as an increasing number of pattern books came to be published during the course of the sixteenth century. Keen needlewomen could buy works such as Shorleykes' *Schoole House for the Needle* and find printed designs suitable for embroidery. The extended title of one volume by Vincentio, published in England by John Wolfe in 1591 clearly demonstrates the use to which such books were to be put: *New and Singular Patternes and Works on Linen serving for patterns to make all sortes of Lace Edgings and Cut workes: Newly invented for the profite and contentment of ladies and gentilwomen and others that are desirous of this Art.*

The format of the seventeenth-century sampler indicates a gradual change in the practical purpose for which it was made. The layout of the motifs is often more ordered, with patterns worked in neat rows. The practice of inscribing the work with the date and the name of the embroideress became more common during this transitional period, which suggests that the finished piece was intended less as a form of reference than as a demonstration of the worker's ability. The fact that some even include the name of the teacher who had instructed the maker shows that they were beginning to be used as schoolroom exercises (plate 10).

Many of the pieces made during the seventeenth century demonstrate the same high standards and levels of technical skill that are to be found in Elizabethan embroidery. The wide variety of stitches used includes satin, chain, buttonhole, eyelet, cross and arrowhead stitches. Cut and drawn thread work was also popular. The embroidery is usually worked on linen in silk threads, occasionally in wool, and in many cases enriched with beads, pearls and gilt threads. Sometimes the details are embroidered in raised work or highlighted with spangles (plate 4).

It seems that most of these samplers were made by children. The quality and range of techniques employed implies that girls were taught to sew at a very early age and expected to practice until they were expert. Since the majority of finished pieces have very few mistakes on them, it seems likely that they were made solely to show off the skill of the young embroideress once she had gained a certain level of proficiency, and that the initial practice and learning was done on other work.

There are two main types of sampler at this period: the 'spot' and the 'band'. The band sampler is normally long and narrow and worked with bands or rows of repeating border designs (plates 7, 8). Many of these are based on earlier pattern books with a strong Italian influence which have illustrations of curving Renaissance-style vines and acanthus leaves. By the seventeenth century, the original designs have often been reduced to more formalized rows of stiff flowering plants or zig-zagging flower heads which point alternately up and down and are connected by stylized stems.

Another popular feature of the band sampler was the use of cut and open work techniques (plate 3). Many of the borders were worked by removing various threads of the linen cloth and weaving over the remaining threads to form an open work grid. The embroideress would then darn over the grid to produce a pattern which stood out against the background mesh, in a technique similar to filet work. There are also many examples of needleweaving, which involved withdrawing all the weft threads from a particular area and binding together the remaining warp threads to form a pattern. A further technique known as reticella, in which the skeleton of the linen forms the framework for a needlepoint design, entails infilling the ground grid with detached buttonhole stitches.

The spot sampler is closer in style to sixteenth-century work and often more attractive than the band sampler. The motifs are set out in a less regimented fashion and many have a naïve charm (plate 2). The material is normally worked all over with a variety of randomly placed spot motifs of naturalistic design or small sections from a geometric border. Carnations, thistles, tulips and vines were very popular, as were stags, birds and butterflies. Insects, too, were among the most attractive and unusual subjects for embroidery during this period, and many embroidered pictures and spot samplers were decorated with carefully drawn caterpillars, exotic bees and creepy-crawlies of all kinds, attesting to a contemporary interest in nature.

Samplers of this kind are rarely signed or dated, but they seem to have been popular throughout the century. Normally more square in shape than the band sampler, they appear to us to display a greater originality in the haphazard placement of the motifs.

Some of the individual designs used on spot samplers recur in embroidered cushions, or worked small purses or pin-cushions. As the seventeenth century progressed, however, the relevance of the designs and stitches being worked on samplers to more general needlework declined. It was no longer fashionable to decorate costume with patterns of this kind, although the borders could be used on household linen. The increasingly outdated nature of sampler work can be seen in the development of cut work. This technique was fashionable in the late sixteenth century for decorating ruffs and cuffs, but by the seventeenth century it was being replaced by more delicate free scrolling lace designs made from needle and bobbin lace. Cut work probably reached a peak of stylistic perfection by around 1615. However, it continues to appear in rows on band samplers throughout the century. The utility of the sampler design was gradually becoming less important.

By the eighteenth century, the original practical purpose had disappeared altogether. The Georgian sampler was really just a decorative piece of needlework. It was nearly square in shape and the practice of dividing the work into bands was, for the most part, abandoned. Borders were common and the overall design balanced a collection of motifs around a central axis and in many cases a verse.

Architectural motifs grew increasingly popular throughout the eighteenth and nineteenth centuries. Large Georgian houses were often worked with a flower garden in front of them, occasionally peopled with figures and animals. Some show actual buildings, or even the embroideress's home. (There is one depicting Milton Lodge 'the seat of S J Astley Bart. Norfolk'.) Others would appear to be imaginary houses, since many of them follow a set design which reappears on several samplers, such as the imaginary Temple of Solomon. There are even representations of the school or orphanage in which the child who did the embroidery was educated. Further popular architectural motifs include windmills, pagodas and classical temples, which would be depicted alongside shepherds and shepherdesses, rows of flowers and birds, and a wide variety of animals, particularly dogs and stags.

The sampler was beginning to become an embroidered picture, a decorative piece intended to be admired and even framed rather than kept in a workbox and used only occasionally. A sampler of 1721 sold recently had the name of the embroideress and the date painted on the original frame by 11-year-old Margaret

Underwood. Jane Austen in *Sense and Sensibility* describes a room in which there 'still hung a landscape in coloured silks of [Charlotte's] performance, in proof of her having spent seven years at a great school in town to some effect'; and while this is clearly a reference to an embroidered picture, by the late eighteenth and early nineteenth centuries the sampler was fulfilling the same function. It was done to reflect the skill of the embroideress and her teacher, and to provide an attractive piece of needlework.

The educative function was now also fulfilled by embroidered verses, many of which formed part of the school curriculum. A large number of them were religious (plate 16), and some dedicated the work to Christ. Others had a high moral tone or considered the transitory nature of life and the inevitability of death, which seem rather morbid subject matter for a child. There are extracts from the Bible: the Ten Commandments, the Psalms and the Lord's Prayer appearing frequently, perhaps as a reflection of the rise of Methodism. *Divine and Moral Songs for Children* by Isaac Watts, which was first published in 1720, and Wesley's 1736 *Hymns* must have provided many verses suitable for samplers.

The increase in the number of embroidered verses on samplers coincides with a decrease in the variety of stitches used. Difficult cut work and complicated techniques such as rococo and rice stitch were gradually abandoned. Children were expected to learn from the alphabets and moralistic verses which formed the content of their work, as much as from the sewing methods involved.

In the late eighteenth century, the range of educational subject matter increased as map samplers became popular. Normally these were worked to show the outlines of England and Wales, with the names of the counties embroidered in coloured silks. However, some more ambitious children worked on the map of Europe (plate 26), or even of the whole world. Many map samplers had naturalistic floral borders and elaborate inscriptions. The figure of Britannia holding her shield was a popular addition to maps of Britain. Many such samplers were commercially prepared with the outlines of the map printed on a white ground ready for immediate work. Printed examples can be found from Carrington Bowles, and Laurie and Whittle. They had the obvious advantage of teaching the schoolgirl geography and needlework while keeping her busy. However, their popularity lasted only a few decades during the late eighteenth and early nineteenth centuries.

Other teaching samplers can be found adorned with multiplication tables (plate 30). There were also novelties, such as the perpetual calendar worked at Walton School in 1781, a rebus sampler made by 10-year-old Elizabeth Bullock in 1793 and an acrostic sampler by Maria Trendell, aged 8, in 1825.

The samplers made during the second half of the eighteenth and the early nineteenth centuries are similar in many ways. The motifs gradually grow a little stiffer and more formalized. Trees begin to look like cut-outs for Christmas cards, and the berry borders become more of a zig-zag pattern and less naturalistic. In the mid-nineteenth century, however, this trend was reversed as embroiderers began to take up Berlin woolwork, in which designs were copied stitch by stitch from patterns originally published in Berlin and worked in brightly coloured wools manufactured in Gotha and dyed in Berlin. The patterns were printed on squared paper, with each square representing one square on the canvas. Although a certain number of such books were to be found in England from 1805 onwards, it was not until 1831 that they were imported in large quantities and became widely available. The effect of this craze on samplers was quite considerable. Berlin woolwork encouraged the depiction of naturalistically shaded motifs (plates 38 and 40). Instead of being conceived as two-dimensional objects, flowers and animals were given an impression of solid form, an impression that does not always work in embroidery. The representation of small landscapes and rustic scenes with peasants and cottages became popular, as did parrots and lush overblown flowers.

As most Berlin woolwork patterns were intended for use on a square meshed canvas and to be sewn in woollen cross or tent stitch, many of the samplers which used their designs are less fine than those worked in silk thread on tammy earlier in the century. They are mainly embroidered in a uniform cross stitch (which came to be known as sampler stitch) and display little technical skill, although they are often attractively decorated.

Another result of the enthusiasm for Berlin woolwork was the development of a new type of sampler, which was long and narrow and often bound with coloured ribbon. It seems to have been used for much the same purposes as the early samplers and was worked in wools in a greater variety of stitches than was common in the schoolroom sampler, with many sections of different patterns and borders. Although the needlewomen who worked them were definitely adults, it is not clear whether they were professionals advertising their skills or amateurs collecting a personal reference library of embroidery.

Another phenomenon of the Victorian era to be reflected in embroidery was the interest in death and mourning. There are many memorial samplers in existence, a large proportion of them American. These normally commemorate the death of a member of the embroideress's family, depict an urn or a tombstone flanked by weeping willows, and include an inscription bearing the name and dates of the deceased. Commemorative samplers of a less gloomy nature were also popular, and were worked to mark an important public event in the same way that handkerchiefs would be printed. Plate 37 shows one example made for the Great Exhibition of 1851, and in Wales samplers were worked depicting the Menai bridge in 1838.

Samplers from the second half of the nineteenth century are comparatively rare. Although schoolroom pieces continued to be made up to the end of the century, they became less popular as Berlin woolwork, which lent itself admirably to sampler work, was replaced in popularity by 'Art Needlework'. This was a more creative form of embroidery, which developed from the influence of William Morris and others like him who were interested in historical embroideries and the revival of needlework as a serious craft. It demanded more imagination and originality from the worker, and so was unsuited to the formalized, stale motifs common on nineteenth-century samplers. The growth of this new form of embroidery may well be linked with the final disappearance of the sampler.

At the present time samplers have become objects for collection rather than pieces to be embroidered. Over recent years the salesrooms have sold works from the United States, Germany, Holland, Sweden, Spain, Mexico and Turkey to a range of buyers from an equally international background, although English and American collectors lead the field. The interest in samplers as historical evidence has never been livelier, and while they may not be regarded strictly speaking as works of art, they do tell us a great deal about the people who made them.

SUSAN MAYOR
DIANA FOWLE
DEPARTMENT OF TEXTILES & FANS
CHRISTIE'S SOUTH KENSINGTON
JULY 1989

PLATE 1

A sampler by Jane Bostocke, 1598. This is the earliest known dated sampler. It is worked with metal threads, silks, pearls and beads in a great variety of stitches. The random disposition of the motifs and various patterns show that the worker probably added to her sampler whenever a new pattern caught her fancy. She has completed a total of twenty-four different border designs and several naturalistic spot motifs, all suitable for domestic embroidery, demonstrating the original reference nature of the early sampler. 17 × 15in. (Courtesy of the Victoria and Albert Museum)

ABCDEFGHIKLMNOPQRSTVWXY IANE KONICKH 1598
ALICE LEE WAS BORNE THE 23 OF NOVEMBER BE
ING TVESDAY IN THE AFTER NOONE 1596

PLATE 2

An early seventeenth-century spot motif sampler. This is worked in coloured silks, with many different pattern samples. They are mainly sections from geometric border patterns, and are scattered randomly over the sampler, unlike the later, more orderly, band samplers. There is also a small embroidered panel, intended to cover a purse or wallet, which is decorated with small flowers almost identical to the one two-thirds of the way down this sampler. This was almost certainly worked by the same person and demonstrates how the seventeenth-century embroiderer copied patterns from her sampler on to other pieces. It is a very good example of the practical nature of the early pieces. 19 × 8in. (Courtesy of Christie's, South Kensington)

PLATE 3

An unfinished sampler dated 1657. This is worked in many-coloured silks with three bands of stylized flowers and a row of letters at the base. These bands were originally derived from Italian pattern books; most of them are based on natural objects such as acorns and flowering plants, although some are geometric. This sampler also has a band of cutwork at the top. 18 × 7in. (Courtesy of the Swamethan Collection)

PLATE 4

An early seventeenth-century sampler depicting three ladies in Tudor dress, the central one possibly intended to represent Queen Elizabeth I. They are placed above bands of patterns, which include trailing tulips and other flowers. There are also spot motifs of animals and figures. This example shows how varied the early samplers were in their techniques and materials, since it is embroidered not only in silks, but also with metal threads, pearls and spangles. Many different stitches are used, including 'purl' work, which was popular at the time and involved working the relevant stitches on a separate frame and applying them later onto the linen ground. 35 × 10in. (Courtesy of Christie's, South Kensington)

PLATE 5

A sampler worked by Suzannah Allens, and dated 1668. This is sewn in shades of green, yellow, blue and pink silk. The worker's name and the date are embroidered at the top above a row of letters. Practice in embroidering alphabets was useful for marking linen and similar household articles. This sampler also has bands of flowers, fruit and foliage. 20 × 8in. (Courtesy of the Swamethan Collection)

PLATE 6

A seventeenth-century sampler embroidered in brightly coloured silks. This is worked with bands of trailing floral patterns and a row of 'boxers' at the base. The boxers are the figures with their arms outstretched in a rather aggressive pose. They are quite common motifs on seventeenth-century samplers and are believed to originate from a sixteenth-century Italian pattern depicting lovers exchanging gifts, which was gradually simplified by series of embroideresses. 21 × 7in. (Courtesy of the Swamethan Collection)

PLATE 7

A seventeenth-century sampler embroidered in many-coloured silks. This is another band sampler worked with rows of patterns suitable for decorating borders, including vines, carnations, trees and a lady in Elizabethan dress. (Courtesy of the Swamethan Collection)

PLATE 8

A late seventeenth-century sampler embroidered in coloured silks. The pious verse demonstrates how by the end of the century samplers were being used not only to teach needlework, but also to impart moral and religious knowledge. This sampler also has a deep band of raised work at the bottom with an elaborate design of flowers and snakes. (Courtesy of the Swamethan Collection)

PLATE 9

A seventeenth-century sampler embroidered in coloured silks. This is worked with a pious verse, alphabets and two bands of floral border patterns. It also has a row of bargello stitch work at the base; this is often called flame stitch as the zig-zag patterns resemble burning fire. In the centre a lady and a gentleman are depicted on either side of a very disproportionately sized plant. (Courtesy of the Swamethan Collection)

PLATE 10

A sampler dated 1691 and embroidered by Elizabeth Meadow. Although the design is not very unusual, consisting mainly of alphabets and border patterns, the inscription is very interesting. The embroideress has worked the name of her teacher or 'dame' Iuda Hayle in the verse. There are in existence five other samplers dating from this period to 1710 which bear the same teacher's name. This group of samplers proves how by the end of the seventeenth-century samplers had become a schoolroom exercise to be worked by children, rather than a reference for adult embroiderers. 21 × 5in. (Courtesy of Christie's, South Kensington)

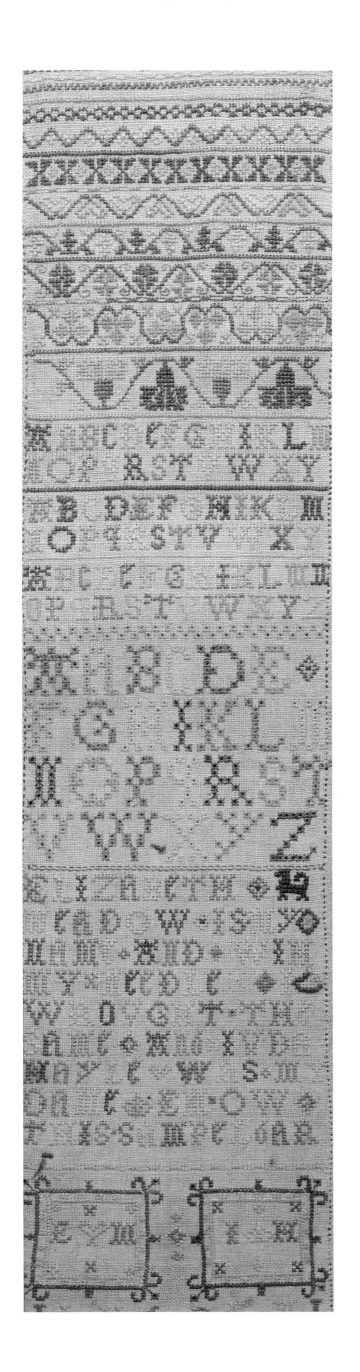

PLATE 11

A sampler dated 1746 and worked in coloured silks. This has four sets of alphabets each worked in differing stitches and several decorative bands. There is a pair of confronting birds just above the date. 17 × 18in. (Courtesy of the Swamethan Collection)

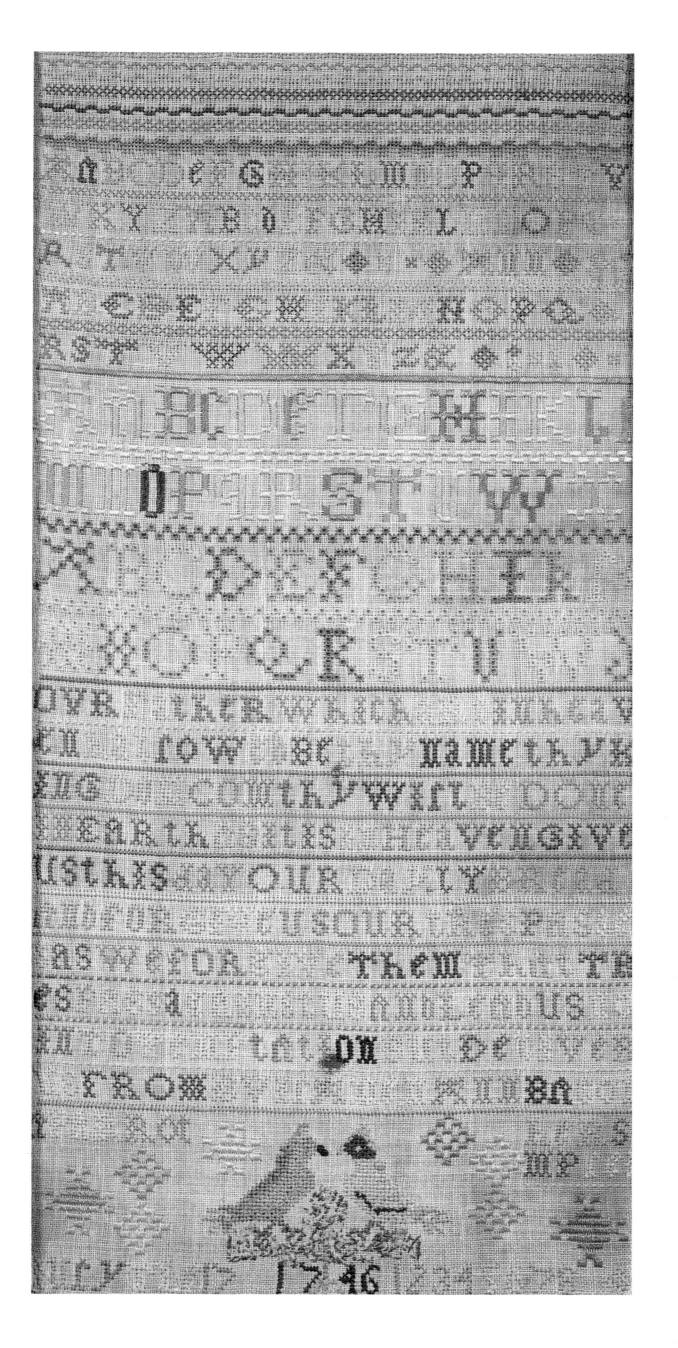

1746

PLATE 12

A sampler dated 1756, embroidered in coloured silks and worked with the names of various members of the Hodsell family. It is also decorated with alphabets, numerals and a religious verse, each row being separated by a thin band of patterns. A very simple sampler, it was probably worked by quite a young girl, possibly even as a first attempt before she was capable of more elaborate needlework. 8 × 13in. (Courtesy of the Swamethan Collection)

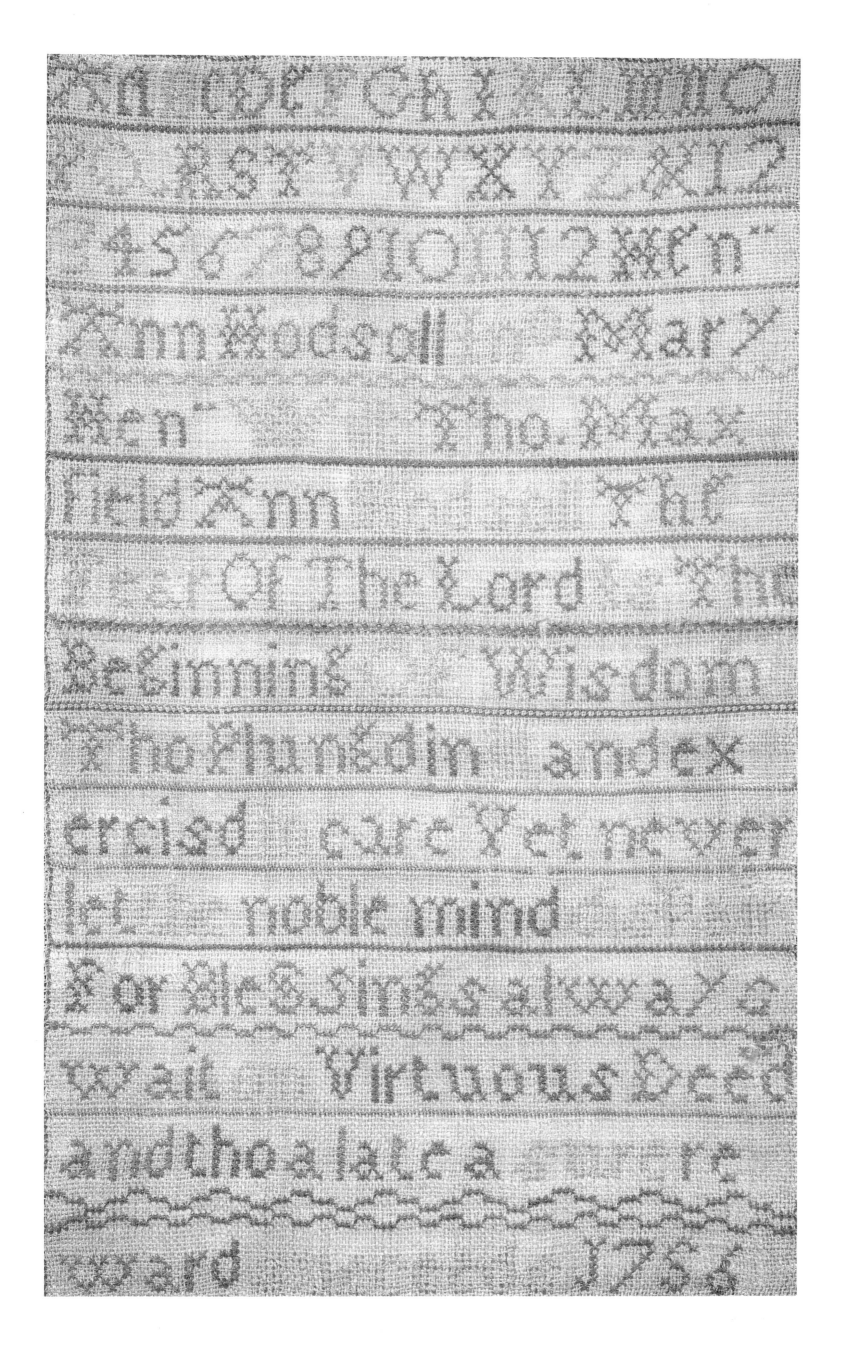

An †…†GH†…†LMnO

…RSTV…WXY…Z…12

456789101112…Mn˜

Ann Hodsall   Mary

Hen˜   Tho Max

field Ann   Th˜

˜ar Of The Lord ˜ The

Beginning   Wisdom

Tho Plundin and ex

ercisd   ˜ur Yet never

let   noble mind

For Blessings alwa˜ a

wait   Virtuous De˜

andtho a late a   re

ward   175˜

PLATE 13

A sampler 'wrought by Mary Portar in the 14 year of her age in the year of our Lord 1770. Youngest daughter of John and Mary Portar of Northsomercoates.' This inscription and other verses and prayers are all in black cross stitch. There is a central panel worked with a flame stitch pattern in coloured silks, and the border is composed of colourful, typically eighteenth-century, naturalistic flowers. Flame stitch was popular at this period and was often used to decorate upholstery and wallets. The section of flame stitch included here shows that Mary Portar's sampler still has some practical value, although it is mainly a decorative piece. 24 × 30in. (Courtesy of the Swamethan Collection)

PLATE 14

A sampler by Margaret Harper, dated 1782. This is embroidered in coloured silks with verses and alphabets. It also has bands of geometric patterns and a flame stitch section similar to that on plate 13. At the base the embroideress has worked a green field decorated with various animals, birds and exotic flowers. The whole sampler is framed by a berry border. This type of border derives from the earlier naturalistic floral forms of edging which were gradually simplified, until by the nineteenth century they are often little more than zig-zag patterns. 20 × 13in. (Courtesy of Christie's, South Kensington)

ABCDEFGHIKLMNOPQRSTUVWXY Z & ÆEOUY

ABCEFGHKLJOPQRSTUVXYZÆ Z X

abcdefghikmnopqrsfsuvwxyz

ABCDEFGHIKLMNOPQ

RSTUVWXYZ Z ÆEIOU

1234567891011 121314 ◊ O that the Sons of men would once be wise
and learn Eternal Happiness to prize ❖

Alexander Harper Elizabeth Harper Sarah Harper
Mary Harper John Harper James Harper Gillis MacBean
Harper Alexander William Harper ◊ James Harper
Anthony Fisher Rachel Fisher Alexander MacBean

Their only great whom no base Motive rules; Reason whole pleasure is
Who owe no Glory to the Breath of Fools The Joys of sense Lies in
Friends to true Merit to their Country dear These words Health ◊
To others kind but to themselves severe Peace and Competence ❖
Quiet in suffering with their Lot content MARGARET HARPER
And careful to improve the Talents lent HER WORK ANNO
Good without Pride tho' humble yet not mean DOMINI 1792
In Danger fearless and in Death serene

PLATE 15

A Scottish sampler by Agnes Moor, Kelso, dated 1789. This is embroidered in coloured silks, with bands of spot motifs, including a man in a ship, bowls of flowers and exotic birds. It is framed by a berry border. There is little difference in format between English and Scottish samplers, although Scottish examples more often list the relatives' initials. However, this is not always the case, and with samplers such as this, it is best to rely on the information given to us by the embroideress, when suggesting a provenance. 13 × 11in. (Courtesy of Christie's, South Kensington)

PLATE 16

A sampler by Elizabeth Kirk who 'work'd this May 1789 in the ninth year of age, Lincoln'. Above this inscription there are several religious verses and below it a panel with the words 'Long live the King and Queen', flanked by two crowns and coats of arms. Below, a small red brick house, set in a field, is slightly dwarfed by the large vases of flowers on either side. The border is composed of various naturalistic spot motifs. The varying scale in this sampler is quite typical; the motifs bear little relation to each other and are not designed to form a coherent or realistic picture, but rather an attractive demonstration of needlework. 18 × 24in. (Courtesy of the Swamethan Collection)

You whose fond wishes do to Heaven aspire
Who make those blest a boade your sole desire
If you are wise and hope that bliss to gain
Use well your time live not an hour in vain
Let not the Morrow your vain thoughts imploy
But think this day the last you shall enjoy

Tis Education forms the youthful mind
just as the Twig is bent the Trees inclind

ELIZABETH KIRK. WORK'D
THIS. MAY 1789 IN THE NINTH
YEAR OF HER AGE. LINCOLN

Long Live The King

AND

QUEEN

PLATE 17

A darning sampler by Mary Anne Ranson, dated 1802. This is embroidered in coloured silks, with five silk crosses showing various darning techniques and four flower sprays. By this period darning samplers were the only type with any practical use, as although they are also attractive pieces, the techniques they demonstrate are useful in everyday domestic mending. 14 × 17in. (Courtesy of the Swamethan Collection)

Mary Ann · Ranson, 1802

PLATE 18

An American sampler by Rebeckah Ingersolls, dated 1803. This is worked in coloured silks on a linen ground, with a central panel containing alphabets, numerals and a verse. It is framed by a floral and trailing vine inner border, with a saw-tooth outer border. Rebeckah Ingersolls was 12 when she worked this sampler and probably came from New England. (Courtesy of Christie's, New York)

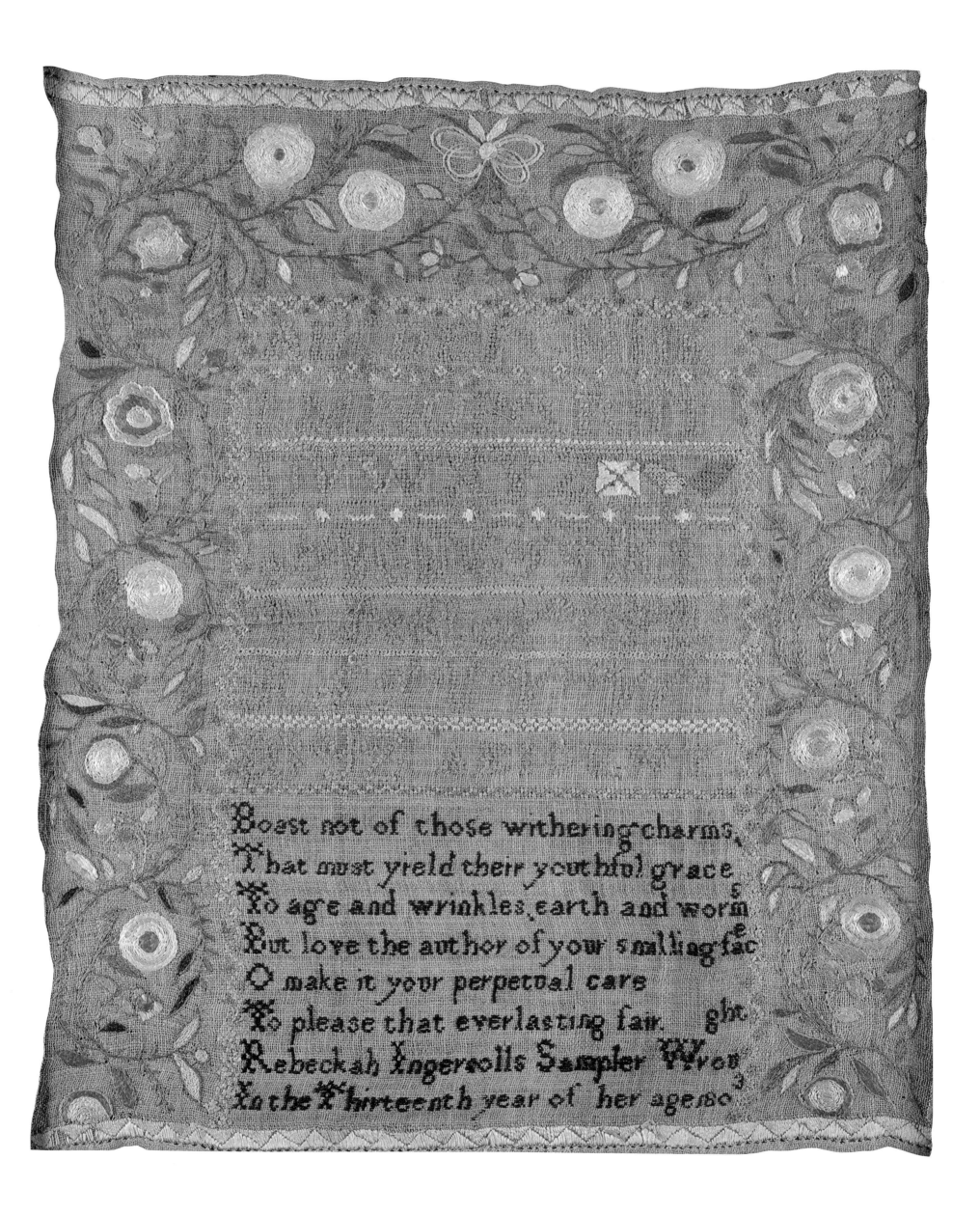

Boast not of those withering charms,
That must yield their youthful grace
To age and wrinkles, earth and worm
But love the author of your smiling fac
O make it your perpetual care
To please that everlasting fair. ght
Rebeckah Ingersolls Sampler Wrou
In the Thirteenth year of her agemo

PLATE 19

A sampler with the inscription 'Phoebe Brown finished this work April 7 1804 at Mrs Venthams Boarding School wrought in her 16 year.' This charming sampler is worked in coloured silks and depicts a realistic farmyard scene. It is a more original subject than the usual formula of this period, which depicts a house flanked by figures and animals. In the foreground there are various animals, a girl feeding chickens and a girl drawing water from a well. The farm buildings and the farmer himself are depicted in the distance. The whole sampler is framed by a floral border. (Courtesy of Christie's, South Kensington)

All you my Friends that now expect to see.
A Piece of Work thus perform'd by me
Cast but A Smile on this my mean endeavour.
I'll strive to mend and be Obedient ever

Phœbe Brown finish'd this Work April 6th 1804 At Mrs Venthams
Boarding School Winton In her 16th Year.

PLATE 20

A sampler worked by Clementina Reddrop, and dated 1804. It is embroidered in coloured silks with an inscription 'these are the spies which went to view the land of Canaan', and depicts the two spies carrying a very large bunch of grapes, flanked by shepherdesses and sheep. At the base there is a small pavilion with the words 'the lord reigneth in Zion'. The whole sampler is within a border of strawberries. 13 × 19in. (Courtesy of the Swamethan Collection)

PLATE 21

A Spanish colonial sampler by Dolores Lohyzo, embroidered in the early nineteenth century in coloured silks. It is worked with narrow half bands of flowers and animals and elaborate geometric patterns. This example is closer in style to the English seventeenth-century samplers than those of the early nineteenth century. (Courtesy of Christie's, South Kensington)

PLATE 22

A sampler by Elizabeth Willets aged 11, dated 1806. Below the religious verse worked in black silk there are two large birds perched on branches, sewn in bright colours. There are also several small flowering plants and bowls of fruit, and a border composed of stylized carnations. These motifs appear quite frequently on samplers of the period, but the finely worked birds are unusual, as they are better drawn and less conventional in form than was normal at the time. 16 × 11in. (Courtesy of the Swamethan Collection)

Hail risen Jesus Hail my Lord and God
I am thy own Redeemed with thy own blood
O Lord what hast thou done thy death and smart
Have got the day have won my very hearts
Beyond my faith and hope and every grace
Ill boast alone of thee my Righteousness.
Thy gifts and streams are sweet & grateful own
But o thou bridegroom dear thou art my crown,

Elizabeth Willetts
Work Aged 11
1806

PLATE 23

A sampler worked in coloured silks, depicting an elaborate landscape with three buildings connected by pathways through fields containing sheep, cows and a milkmaid. Above this is a religious verse surrounded by various flowers. The border consists of zig-zagging carnations. There is a separate inscription which reads 'This work done by Harriet Couch in the year 1812, aged eight'. Most samplers were worked by children between the ages of 10 and 15; Harriet Couch was very young to have sewn such a technically skilled sampler depicting such an unusually complicated landscape. 14 × 13in. (Courtesy of the Swamethan Collection)

Exonerate your Mind of Worthy Cares
Spend each Lords Day in Spiritual Affairs
Such Wretched Souls as Squander that a way
Repent it Sorely at their Dying Day

A sampler worked by Mary Graham, aged 15, and dated 1812. This is embroidered with bands of alphabets, numerals and trailing floral patterns. The main band consists of bowls of carnations flanked by crowns, birds and fruit. These border patterns are derived from those on seventeenth-century samplers, but by this date it is extremely unlikely that they were ever used on any other piece of needlework, as their function here is purely decorative rather than practical. 12 × 14in. (Courtesy of Christie's, South Kensington)

PLATE 25

An American sampler worked by Elisabeth Stewart Fraserburgh, and dated March 1812. It is sewn in many-coloured silks on a linen ground. The verse, entitled 'On Virtue', is placed above a large classical mansion set on a lawn and flanked by trees. The top of the sampler is decorated with an elaborate floral swag. The design is typical of English samplers and demonstrates that the two countries often produced similar works with the same basic formulas. 16 × 12in. (Courtesy of Christie's, New York)

ON VIRTUE

Virtue is the chiefest beauty of the mind
The noblest ornament of humankind
Virtue is our safeguard and our guiding star
That stirs up reason when our senses err

PLATE 26

A map sampler depicting 'A new map of Europe, 1812'. This is embroidered in shaded brown chenille thread and black silks on an ivory silk ground. The place names are in black and the borders in pale colours. There is a scale in the bottom right-hand corner. This piece is interesting as a historical guide to the national borders during the period directly before the battle of Waterloo. 18 × 21in. (Courtesy of the Swamethan Collection)

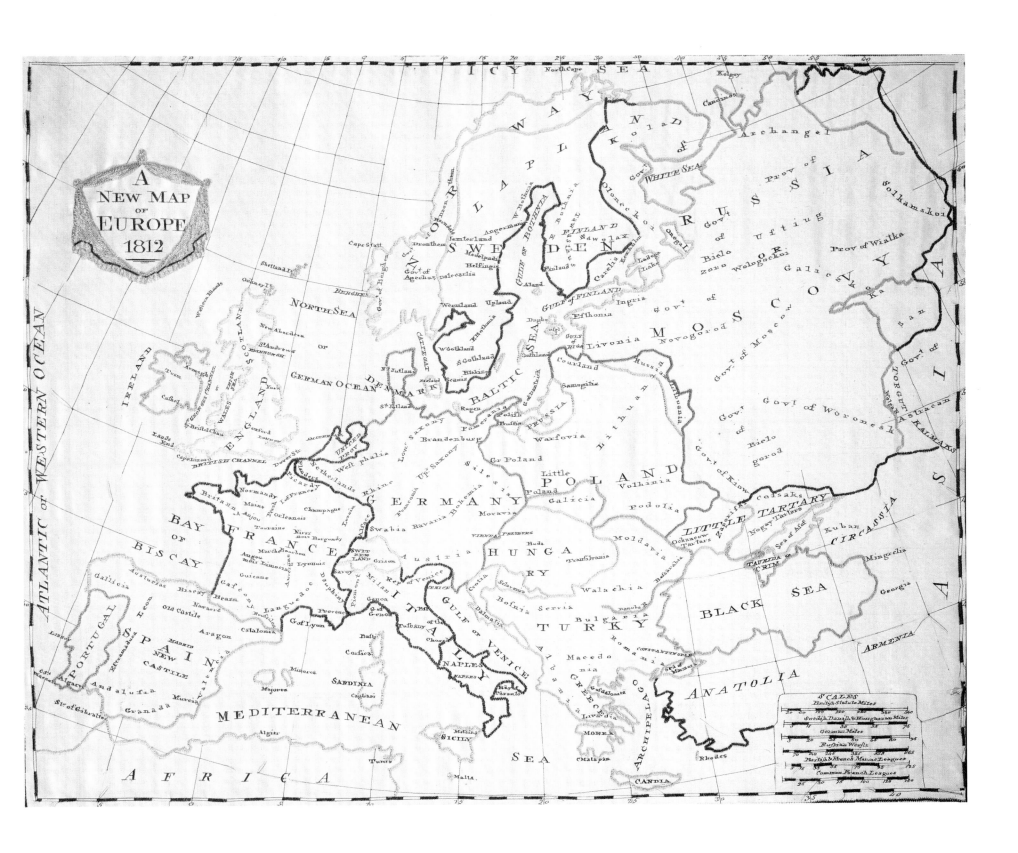

A
NEW MAP
OF
EUROPE
1812

ICY SEA

ATLANTIC or WESTERN OCEAN

NORTH CAPE

NORWAY

LAPLAND

SWEDEN

GULF OF BOTHNIA

FINLAND

WHITE SEA

RUSSIA

Archangel

Prov of Solikamskoi

Prov of Wiatka

GULF of FINLAND

BALTIC SEA

Livonia

MOSCOW

Govt of Woronesh

CIRCASSIA

IRELAND

SCOTLAND

ENGLAND

WALES

NORTH SEA

GERMAN OCEAN

DENMARK

BRITISH CHANNEL

UNITED PROV

Netherlands

Westphalia

PRUSSIA

Brandenburg

Warsovia

LITHUA

POLAND

Little Poland

Volhinia

Podolia

LITTLE TARTARY

GERMANY

Silesia

Galicia

Moravia

Bohemia

Bavaria

Swabia

Austria

HUNGARY

Transilvania

Moldavia

BLACK SEA

BAY OF BISCAY

FRANCE

Normandy

Britain

Maine

Anjou

Orleanois

Champagne

Lorrain

Burgundy

SWITZERLAND

Dauphiny

Provence

Savoy

Piedmont

Milan

Genoa

GULF OF VENICE

VENICE

Croatia

Dalmatia

Bosnia

Servia

Bulgaria

Walachia

Romania

CONSTANTINOPLE

TURKY

ANATOLIA

ARMENIA

PORTUGAL

SPAIN

NEW CASTILE

Andalusia

Granada

Str of Gibraltar

G. of Lyon

Corsica

SARDINIA

Majorca

Minorca

ITALY

Tuscany

NAPLES

SICILY

MEDITERRANEAN SEA

Malta

GREECE

Macedonia

ARCHIPELAGO

CANDIA

Rhodes

AFRICA

SCALES
British Statute Miles
Swedish, Danish, & Hungarian Miles
German Miles
Russian Wersts
British & French Marine Leagues
Common French Leagues

PLATE 27

A sampler worked by Elizabeth Smith, and dated 1814. This is sewn in coloured silks and depicts a farmyard scene consisting of a small house, with fields in the foreground and a flower garden. Above this there are several spot motifs, including one of sailing boats on a wavy sea. There is a religious verse at the top and the whole is framed by a formalized floral border. This sampler is worked with several unusual motifs; the ships and hanging tassels are quite rare, as is the naturalistic horse. Animals are normally less realistically drawn on samplers. 26 × 19in. (Courtesy of the Swamethan Collection)

Christ dwells in Heaven but visits on Earth Cant vi 1 2 13

When strangers faint and hear me tell
What beauties in my Saviour dwell.
Where is he gone, they fain would know
That they may seek and love him too

My best beloved keeps his throne
On hills of light in worlds unknown
But he defcends, and fhows his face
In the young gardens of his grace.

In vineyards planted by his hand,
Where fruitful trees in order stand.
He feeds among the fpicy beds,
Where lilies fhow their spotlefs heads.

He has engrofs'd my warmest love
No earthly charms my Soul can move:
I have a mansion in his heart,
Nor death nor hell shall make us part

He takes my soul e'er I'm aware
And fhows me where his glories are,
No chariot of Amminadib
The heavenly rapture can describe.

O may my spirit daily rise
On wings of faith above the skies
Till death shall make my last remove
To dwell for ever with my love.

Elizabeth Smith Her Work

aged 14 Years 18 14

PLATE 28

A sampler worked by Ann Garness, in 1820. The religious verse and the alphabets are in black silk. The rest of the sampler is embroidered in polychrome silks. At the base an exotic bird is depicted perched on a cherry tree branch surrounded by bowls of fruit. There are also two large vases containing roses and foliage. Both these features are slightly unusual and very finely worked. The trailing carnations and honeysuckle border are more typical and are seen on many samplers of the period. 21 × 13in. (Courtesy of Christie's, South Kensington)

ABCDEFGHIJKLMNOPQRSTUVWXYZ&12

abcdefghiklmnopqrstuvwxyz&1234567891011121314151617181920 21

Character of Christ.
Behold, where, in a mortal form,
Appears each grace divine;
The virtues, all in Jesus meet,
With mildest radiance shine.

Lowly in heart, by all his friends,
A friend and servant found; tears
He wash'd their feet, he wip'd their
And heal'd each bleeding wound.

Be Christ my pattern and my guide:
His Image may I bear:
O may I tread his sacred steps,
And his bright glories share.

Ann Garness   June 16 1826

PLATE 29

A Spanish sampler by Antonia Castillo, dated 1829. The inscription states that the sampler was worked at the Free School in Cadiz, under the direction of Dona Joaquina Sanchez. It is sewn in coloured silks with vases of flowers along the base and small trailing patterns between each line of the inscription. The border is of Greek fret pattern. 15 × 11in. (Courtesy of the Swamethan Collection)

PLATE 30

*An early nineteenth-century Scottish sampler, probably embroi-
dered by J.M.C. This example is very plain and was made as a
schoolroom exercise with the aim of teaching the worker her
multiplication tables and basic needlework, rather than to be
admired as a decorative piece. It was worked at the Duchess of
Athole's School. (Courtesy of the Swamethan Collection)*

MULTIPLICATION TABLE

1	2	3	4	5	6	7	8	9	10	11	12
2	4	6	8	10	12	14	16	18	20	22	24
3	6	9	12	15	18	21	24	27	30	33	36
4	8	12	16	20	24	28	32	36	40	44	48
5	10	15	20	25	30	35	40	45	50	55	60
6	12	18	24	30	36	42	48	54	60	66	72
7	14	21	28	35	42	49	56	63	70	77	84
8	16	24	32	40	48	56	64	72	80	88	96
9	18	27	36	45	54	63	72	81	90	99	108
10	20	30	40	50	60	70	80	90	100	110	120
11	22	33	44	55	66	77	88	99	110	121	132
12	24	36	48	60	72	84	96	108	120	132	144

J MC K. Duchess of Athole's
School.

PLATE 31

A sampler embroidered by Rachel de la Rue and dated 1828. Unlike most samplers of its period this example has no religious verse, but only the date and embroideress's name. However, the red brick house flanked by small figures and trees is very typical, as are the pots of carnations and the bowls of fruit which appear on nearly all nineteenth-century samplers. 24 × 23in. (Courtesy of Christie's, South Kensington)

PLATE 32

A sampler by Eliza Wagg, aged 10, dated 1833. This is worked in silks with a verse, 'Jesus Permit', which was very popular at this period and frequently appears on samplers. Below the verse there is a red brick house and a smaller gazebo placed among trees and lawns, and several small spot motifs at the bottom. The border is composed of formalized flowers. 15in square. (Courtesy of the Swamethan Collection)

PLATE 33

A sampler worked by Sarah Wooldridge, aged 10, and dated 1842. The verse is quite small on this sampler and is surrounded by an elaborate border worked with large vines, strawberries, cornucopiae and many flowers, including tulips and chrysanthemums. These motifs are squeezed into any available space and the result is a feeling of overcrowding and asymmetry. The design on nearly all samplers, except the early seventeenth-century ones, is strongly symmetrical, and this piece is unusual in breaking this rule. 16 × 19in. (Courtesy of the Swamethan Collection)

The morning flowers display their sweets
And gay their silken leaves unfold,
As careless of the noontide heats,
As fearless of the evening cold.
Nipt by the wind's unkindly blast,
Parch'd by the sun's directer ray,
The mometary glories waste,
The short lived beauties die away.

Sarah Wooldridges Work Aged 10
1842

PLATE 34

A sampler by Mary Ann Beard, dated 1842. The lower half depicts a Palladian red brick mansion, with a lawn in the front of the building and a row of ducks and fruit trees. The house could perhaps be the embroideress's home, or a local house, as real buildings were often depicted on samplers of the period. The embroideress was probably quite young when she made this sampler, as it is not as finely worked as many others. 16in square. (Courtesy of the Swamethan Collection)

PLATE 35

An American sampler by Caroline Hite, Pennsylvania, dated 1841. This is worked in coloured silks and depicts George Washington on horseback. It is copied from an etching of Washington crossing the Delaware printed in New York in 1833. The one other known sampler copied from the same source is also dated 1841. There are a few scattered spot motifs and the whole is framed by a floral border. 16 × 18in. (Courtesy of Christie's, New York)

Caroline Bites Work
In the year 1841 aged
years 2nd 1 month
was born august the
20th 182

God Will my naked soul
Receiv When seperate
From the flesh and break
The Prison of the grave
To raise my bones afresh

Washington
crossing the Deleware

PLATE 36

A mid nineteenth-century sampler by Margaret Winkley aged 9 years. The religious verse is worked in black silk. Beneath this there is a large country house sewn in many colours with cows, trees, plants and a beehive. The border and the various butterflies and birds are worked in chenille threads, a form of embroidery relatively unusual on samplers, although it was often used in embroidered pictures during the eighteenth and nineteenth centuries. Chenille is a thick, fluffy silk, which takes its name from the French word for caterpillar. 27 × 22in. (Courtesy of the Swamethan Collection)

RELIGION is the Chief concern*
Of Mortals here below;
May I its great Importance learn
Its Sov'reign virtue know.

Religion Should our thoughts Engage
Amidst our Youthful bloom,
'Twill fit us for Declining age,
Or for the awful Tomb.

Oh, let us fly— to JESUS fly,
Whose Powerful arm can Save,
Then Shall our hopes ascend on high,
And Triumph o'er the Grave.

Margaret Winkley Aged 9 Years.

PLATE 37

A sampler worked by Mary Pearson, and dated 1851. This example is embroidered in coloured wools and commemorates the Great Exhibition of 1851. The embroideress has accurately depicted the Crystal Palace, the large glass building where the exhibition was held. The border is composed of naturalistic roses and foliage and shows the influence of the fashion for Berlin woolwork. 26 × 24in. (Courtesy of Christie's, South Kensington)

Mary Pearson

1851

A sampler worked by Mary Diggle aged 11 years, and dated 1852. This sampler was embroidered to commemorate the birth in 1851 of the twins William and Emma Compton who are depicted holding hands and gazing up to heaven. They are placed above the verse which praises the pleasures of being a twin. The border is composed of flowers and scrolling motifs. This sampler is very representative of Victorian needlework; it is sewn in brightly coloured wools and the motifs are worked so as to give an impression of their three-dimensional quality. (Courtesy of Christie's, South Kensington)

William and Emma Crompton
Born May 11th 1851

Two sweet children, girl and boy
Shared each other's tears and joy,
They were ever side by side,
Like the Graces beautified.
Form without and thought within
Linked them by the name of twin
For the lips which smiled and burned
With the children's kiss returned.

Mary Diggle Aged 11 yrs 1852

Stand   National   School

PLATE 39

A sampler by M.A. Wrighton, dated 1878. This sampler is rather sad; the embroideress lived in the South Wing of the New Orphan House at Ashley Down in Bristol. She has worked a verse of 'Home Sweet Home' in the centre of the piece. Around the verse there is a series of delicate trailing patterns and alphabets. 15 × 11in. (Courtesy of the Swamethan Collection)

Home Sweet Home

Mid pleasures and palaces
though we may roam

Be it ever so humble there's
no place like Home

M A Wrighton
South Wing,
New Orphan House
Ashley Down
Bristol
1878

PLATE 40

A sampler by Mary Ann Randell, aged 10, dated 1886. Like most samplers from the second half of the nineteenth century, this is worked in brightly coloured wools and is nearly square in shape, rather than rectangular. It depicts many spot motifs of flowering plants, a house, two small cottages and elaborate birds, and is framed by a simple berry border. (Courtesy of Christie's, South Kensington)